paper planes

Mud Puddle inc.
NEW YORK

by brandon hansen
and kris lightfoot

Copyright © 2007 by
Mud Puddle, Inc.
36 W. 25th Street
New York, NY 10010
info@mudpuddleinc.com

ISBN: 978-1-60311-036-5

Printed in China

table of contents

introduction

All You Need:
A piece of 8½ X 11″ (A4) lightweight paper
A smooth surface

Note: photocopy, printer, and scrapbook paper will all work. Do not use binder paper with lines – it is too light, and cardstock is too heavy.

IMPORTANT NOTES

Perfect Folds

Paper planes that actually fly must begin with perfect folds. Take your time, measure accurately, line up edges, crease neatly and firmly.

Symmetry

Every paper plane must be exactly the same on both sides. The right wing must be a mirror image of the left wing or your plane will either not fly straight or not fly at all. If you make a mistake on the first side of your airplane make the same mistake on the second side. If the first side is perfect and you make a mistake on the second side, throw away your piece of paper and start again!

THE THROW

The first two or three throws with any paper airplane must be light and breezy. No matter how perfect your folds are or how good your symmetry is, if you throw too hard in the beginning your plane will crash! Once it begins flying the way you think it should, then you can throw as hard and as far as you want to.

Throw, Check, & Tweak

If you cannot get your plane to fly just right take a minute and check the folds, the symmetry, the dihedral (wing angle) (see page 7), as well as the elevators and ailerons (see page 7). The best way to check your plane is to hold your plane up to your eye and stare right down the middle. This will help you make sure you have made all of the folds the same on both sides and that the wings angle upward.

Second Try

If you cannot make your plane fly, regardless of how perfect it looks, take a deep breath, and make a second plane from a different piece of paper. Sometimes there is just no explaining it – certain paper airplanes just will not fly!

FOLDING & TWEAKING

1. Aligning

Most of the planes in this book require folds that are edge-to-edge, corner-to-corner, or edge-to-crease folds. When you make these folds, make sure you put the paper exactly where it is supposed to go. Even a slightly crooked fold will make a difference.

2. Creasing

Every fold must be creased and creased well. First, run your finger from the middle of the fold to one end, then repeat to the other end. Next, check your alignment to make sure all of the edges are where they are supposed to be. Now run back over the top of the crease with your fingernail – again beginning in the center and creasing to one end, then repeat to the other end.

3. Smoothing

Whenever a paper airplane has several folds you will notice after one or two folds that your paper will begin to bubble up or bulge. It is best if you flatten these the minute you notice them. To do this, use a pencil, a dowel, or a bone folder* to sweep over the bulge with enough pressure that the bulge is eliminated.

*Bone Folders, used specifically for creasing paper, are commonly available in stationary, craft and art stores.

PARTS OF THE PAPER AIRPLANE

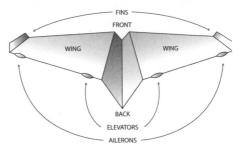

Dihedral

The angle between a plane's wings is what an engineer will call the "Dihedral". Every winged airplane flies best with a positive dihedral, which means that your plane must look like this when you look at it from the tail.

Elevators

The small flaps in a plane's wings that make the plane go up and down are the "Elevators". A plane with up elevators will fly higher and longer, while a plane with down elevators will prevent a plane from flying too high and diving. (Refer to diagram above.)

Ailerons

Ailerons look just like elevators but are at the ends of the wings, not in the middle. An aileron will make a plane bank or roll. An aileron in the right wing of a plane will make it bank and turn left, an aileron in the left wing makes it bank and turn right. (Refer to diagram above.)

the ROCKET

1

Lay paper horizontally on tabletop, fold paper in half lengthwise, crease, unfold.

2

Fold upper left edge corner of paper to meet center fold, crease. Repeat with lower left-hand corner.

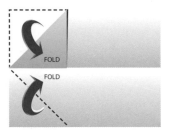

FOLD

FOLD

3

Your plane should look like this:

4 Fold corners over again, so they meet in the middle.

FOLD

FOLD

5 Your plane should look like this:

6 Now you can make some final folds to prepare this plane for flight. Fold along the dotted lines shown in the diagram to give your plane a personal touch. Now go give it a test flight!

Tip: Don't throw this one too hard. A gentle to medium-strength launch is fine.

swing wing

1 Lay paper vertically on tabletop, fold paper in half top to bottom, crease.

FOLD

2 Fold right corner of top layer outward so that it meets center fold, crease.

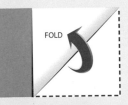
FOLD

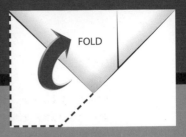

3 Repeat Step 2 with left corner. The top layer, should now look like an inverted triangle.

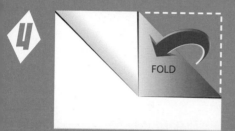

4 Fold the upper right-hand corner down to meet the tip of the triangle, crease. Repeat with upper left-hand corner, unfold.

FOLD

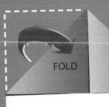

FOLD

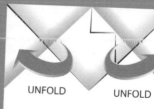

UNFOLD   UNFOLD

Tip: Point this plane straight ahead and use a good hard throw.

5

Fold the right-hand corner to meet the crease you made in Step 4, crease. Repeat with left-hand corner.

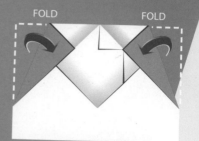

FOLD   FOLD

6

Refold on right-hand side to meet crease made in Step 4, crease. Repeat with left-hand side.

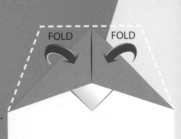

FOLD   FOLD

7

Fold the small triangle peeking out under the folds up over the center, crease, flip over.

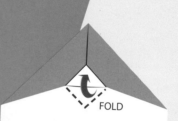

FOLD

FLIP OVER

8 Fold in half from left to right.

Note: Make sure all of the edges line up before you crease your fold.

FOLD

9 Fold the top wing down along the AB line, crease, flip over.

A

FOLD

B

FLIP OVER

10 Fold the second wing on top of the first.

FOLD

Note: Line up edges very carefully.

11 Unfold both wings so that your plane looks like this from the tail section:

12

Make fins on both wings by folding the ends of the wings about 1/2" (1.27 cm) from the end of the wing.

Pilot's Secret:

For big, arching loops, increase the elevators on the back edge of the plane and throw straight towards the sky.

For a slow long glide, flatten the fins.

For dart-like flights, flatten the elevators and stick fins straight up.

the stealth

1

Lay paper vertically on tabletop, fold paper in half lengthwise, crease, unfold.

2

FOLD   UNFOLD

Fold paper in half, crease, unfold.

FLIP OVER

4

Fold the upper-right corner down so that the edge sits on the center crease, crease. Repeat with left side.

FOLD   FOLD

5

FOLD

Fold the top point down so that it meets the 2 creases at the very center point.

6

Fold the upper-left corner so that the right edge of the paper begins where the fold of the triangle is, crease...

...unfold...

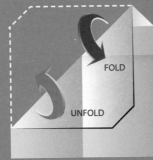

FOLD

UNFOLD

Repeat with upper-right side.

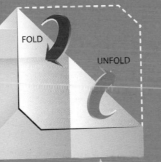

FOLD

UNFOLD

Tip: To fly this plane, cock your arm back and throw it slightly toward the ground.

7 Place paper flat and pull up (where the diagram shows the red arrows) on both sides of the paper moving the red arrows toward each other.

8 The red arrow edges will fold down into the middle crease and rest together on the fold of the middle crease.

9 Fold the inner triangle up and inside.

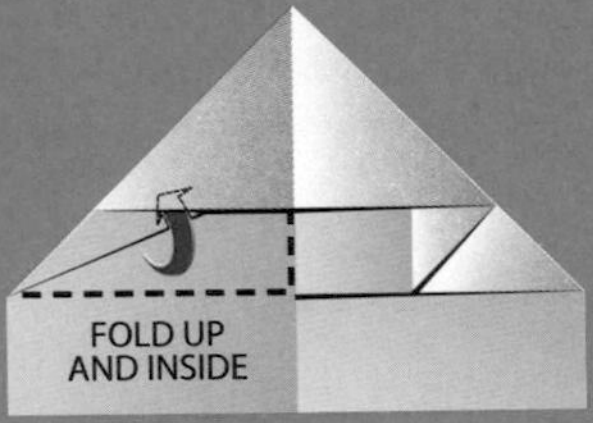

Repeat for right side.

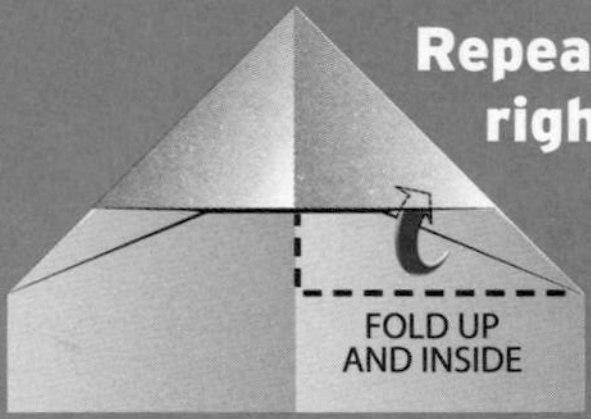

FOLD UP AND INSIDE

FOLD UP AND INSIDE

10 Fold on dotted lines to finish.

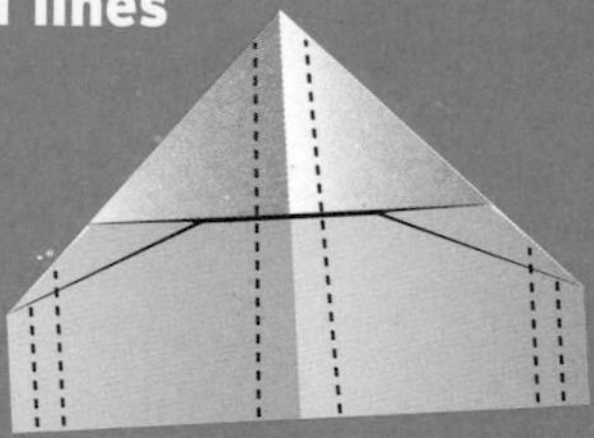

wide wing

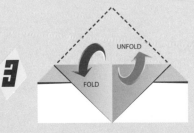

1 Lay paper horizontally on tabletop, fold in half widthwise, crease, unfold.

2 Fold top two corners to meet center fold line, crease.

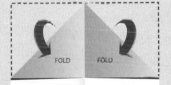

FOLD   FOLD

3

UNFOLD

FOLD

Fold top triangle down over center to meet lower edge, crease, unfold.

Fold point to meet crease made in Step 3, crease.

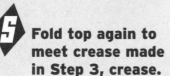

Fold top again to meet crease made in Step 3, crease.

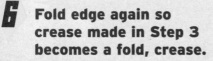

Fold edge again so crease made in Step 3 becomes a fold, crease.

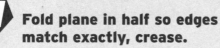

Fold plane in half so edges match exactly, crease.

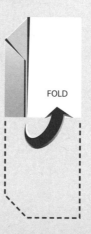

About 1" (2.5 cm) from center fold, fold each wing, crease.

Note: Make sure wings line up.

 Fold up edges of wings about 1" (2.5 cm) from the end of the wings.

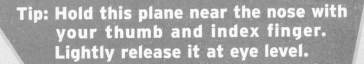

Tip: Hold this plane near the nose with your thumb and index finger. Lightly release it at eye level.

the ski plane

1 Lay paper vertically on tabletop, fold paper in half lengthwise, crease, unfold.

2 Fold right edge of paper to meet center fold, crease. Repeat with left edge, unfold.

FOLD

UNFOLD

3 Fold right edge of paper to meet the first crease on the left-hand side. This creates a fold that is in the center of section A. Crease, unfold.

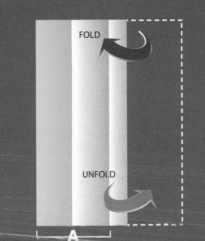

FOLD

UNFOLD

A

Tip: This airplane requires strong paper than normal paper airplanes to increase stability.

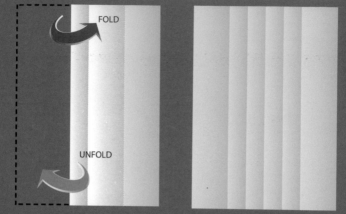

FOLD

UNFOLD

4

FOLD

↕ ABOUT 1" or 1½"

Fold paper so that the top edge is about 1" (2.5 cm) from the bottom edge of the paper.

5

FOLD   FOLD

UNFOLD   UNFOLD

Fold upper right-hand corner so that edge meets first fold, crease, unfold. Repeat with upper left-hand corner.

Step 5 unfolded. Prepare for Step 6 by grabbing a hold of the top paper at point A.

6 As you hold point A, swing and fold it under until point A meets point B. Then take point C and repeat until it meets point B. Make sure your plane looks like the diagram to the right.

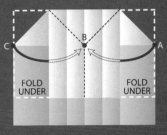

4 Fold the middle section up and crease it.

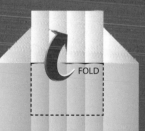

8 In the small square area at the top, fold each corner diagonally so that the vertical edge is lined up with the first crease lines on each side, crease.

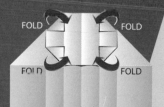

9 Flip plane over.

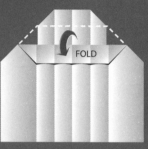

FLIP OVER

10 Fold top part over to meet with the bottom of the upper triangle shape.

FOLD

11 Flip plane over.

FLIP OVER

12 Fold the plane in half along the middle crease line and crease it.

FOLD IN HALF

13 Fold the top fin down to line up with the next crease down. Repeat for other side.

FOLD

 **Fold the wing down along the bottom crease.**

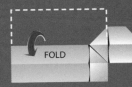 **Flip plane over...** ...and fold the wing down along bottom crease to match other folded wing.

 **Fold lower nose section diagonally to middle crease, unfold.**

Fold lower nose section diagonally inside middle section.

 Fold upper nose section inside middle section. Repeat for other side. You are now finished folding the Ski Plane. Try it out and see how it flies.

the starship

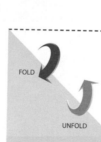

...crease, unfold. Repeat with upper left-hand corner.

1

PICK UP THIS CORNER AND PUT IT NEAR THE **X**.

X

FOLD

UNFOLD

FOLD

UNFOLD

Place paper vertically on tabletop. Mark X on lower left-hand side of the page to about 2" (5 cm) from the bottom. Fold upper right-hand corner to meet the X.

quatro

2 Flip your paper over. Fold the top of the paper down and match the corners with the bottom of the creased X, crease, unfold.

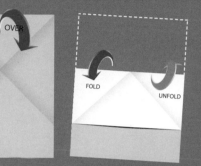

3 Flip the paper over and lay it flat on the tabletop. Press the middle of the creased X and push up the sides where indicated by the red arrows in the diagram. Fold the top over.

Tip: Aim this plane anywhere starting at eye level up and give a good hard throw.

4

Pull the top edge of the paper toward the center, making the sides of the paper fold inward along the horizontal crease, crease.

5

FOLD

Fold the bottom-right corner of the top layer of the triangle to meet the bottom-left corner of the triangle, crease.

6 Fold the new bottom-right corner of the triangle in so that the fold is from the top of the triangle to the lower-right corner of the paper, crease.

FOLD

7

FLIP OVER

Flip the paper over, then fold the top flap of the right side of the paper in half. Crease new fold.

FOLD

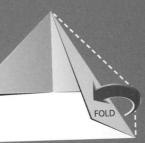

Note: Make sure bottom edges are perfectly lined up.

8 Repeat Step 6 with the left-hand corner, crease, unfold.

Note: Make sure the left fold is directly on top of the right fold.

FOLD

9 Fold triangle down so that the point is on the center crease about 1" (2.5 cm) from the bottom, crease.

FOLD

1"

10 Fold the same triangle up so the point is in the center crease at the top of the paper, crease.

FOLD

FLIP OVER

11 Fold the paper in half from left to right, crease.

Note: Make sure the edges are lined up.

FOLD

12 Fold the paper at a sharp angle on line AB, crease. This is now the wing.

A

FOLD

B

Note: The tail should be approximately twice the size of the nose.

The edge of the wing and the body should be parallel.

13 Flip the paper over, repeat Step 12 folding the second wing lining it up with the first, crease, unfold.

FOLD

14 Your plane should look like this from the tail: